INTO THE LIGHT

INTO THE LIGHT

a collection of poems about love and self-discovery

Daniela Koulikov

First published in 2026.

Cover design by Daniela Koulikov.

For my mum.

Thank you for always believing in me.

Table of Contents

you were a shooting star

dazzling

and yet

only passing through my sky.

Part I

The Stars

tell me nice things

do you think we were always meant to be,

red thread from heaven pulling us in?

when you first saw me,

did any part of you burn with recognition?

was everything else worth it,

just for us to meet?

when the sun sets tonight and

rises tomorrow,

will you feel the same way?

I know you don't believe in fate or
soulmates

but it's a cold night,

so would you mind humouring me?

or should we just keep talking about

the books we'd like to read,

the way I always lose my bookmarks?

if you keep looking at me like that,

I might forget how to say anything at all.

sailor's delight

balcony door open,

spring breeze sweet and mellow

warmth on my tongue,

tidings of good days to follow

step outside,

soak in the fading light

red scattered through clouds

sailor's delight

if I were to make a list of obsessions,

you would be first every time.

I think of little else,

your hands, kind eyes, on repeat.

just be gentle, please,

you smile, you always do,

reply, so sweetly,

with you,

I always am.

espresso martinis all night long

dimly lit, gentle jazz, cocktail half drunk

you tell me about your day

but if we're being honest,

and I'd like to be honest with you,

I mostly watch.

you falter in your story

lost your train of thought.

you change the subject:

what do I think of the bar?

the bar is a pleasant discovery,

but honestly, I'd go anywhere with you.

just say yes

what do you dream about?

my hands on you,

legs twisting the sheets,

or us at the kitchen table,

having breakfast and coffee?

which of those dreams

is more intimate,

would you say?

summer nectar

mango juice drips down my fingers, wrists,
chin

heat radiates through the car window

sand in the car, in our shoes

hot nights where the sheets stick to you

sunlight kissing my skin,

dress hitched high on my thighs, bronzed
and

sticky

you sing along to the music,

hard to pay attention,

air is hot and dry and presses against our skin,

you change the song and I have this urge to

kiss you

you see me looking and you laugh

a red light, you pull me in,

lick the mango juice off my face and I squeal

we're almost at the beach, you say, reading my mind

(when did you get so good at that?)

you say it'll be worth the wait,

the water will be vibrant blue, crystal clear.

I hum in agreement and give in,

lounge back in the passenger seat, close my eyes,

feel the breeze on my cheeks, my eyelashes.

I tell you,

I'll trust you, this time (and next time, and the time after that)

I love you (today and tomorrow and the day after that)

no more broken hearts (you promised)

even with my eyes closed, I know you smile

(isn't that the beauty of knowing you like the back of my hand?)

dreaming

let's go to the market together,

oat lattes, fresh groceries,

overpriced pastries.

let's spend rainy days together,

making pizzas from scratch,

laughing ourselves silly.

let's go everywhere together

oversleep, go for a long walk,

a skinny dip in the deep blue,

share a bottle of wine in the sand,

Riesling or Sav Blanc,

I promise this time I won't mind.

have the bad days together too,

storming outside and in

arguments and eggshells and

twelve missed calls

we say things we don't mean

and don't ask questions

that we should

we make up and

those days I promise

to love you through the good and the bad.

needlework

there is a thread between us

at first, loosely tied, now worked into an
art of embroidery.

do you feel the pull of it,

when the afternoon sun illuminates my
lounge

and I read your favourite book on my
couch?

there is a dream between us

bluebells & coastal visits

salt on our lips

a happy home & a nursery &

buzzing bees

there is a fear between us

inexplicable thoughts of dissolving into
you,

loving you into oblivion,

you ask if I will still love you if I know
every inch of you

I will

I'll thread my fingers with yours

and promise I won't let go.

there is a love between us

bone-achingly deep,

tender & endless.

come back home

sprawled across my bed,

stars inch across the sky

cars race on streets below

crickets chirp in a sea of white noise

I'd like to live in this moment forever

intertwined with

the gentle beat of your heart

the whirl of my ceiling fan

avoiding counting the nights

before you leave

months later I will be

sprawled across my bed

alone

watching the stars

alone

wondering if you can see

the same stars as me.

I tell you that I love you

you kiss me and

you taste like home.

six long months

six long months of

missing you, of

longing

six long months and

twenty-four hours of travel in

four airports with

two suitcases

six long months and

you have changed

and

so have I

six long months for

three short

blissful weeks

six long months to

plant a sunflower seed

three short weeks to

watch it grow and

find the sun.

a million silver stitches,

the pattern no longer makes sense.

a shooting star that has cooled in my
palms,

an effervescent moon in the sky.

it asks,

what will it cost to transform?

will it cost more to stay the same?

Part II

The Moon

labyrinth

you hand me a thread,

say it will lead me out.

into the maze I go.

what awaits me,

I do not know.

in the middle,

        a monster, perhaps

        so sly,

        my name on its tongue

no torch, only trust,

and the dark,

tangled thread in my hand.

at last, the moon shows

a silver flash

I follow with hope.

out of your maze,

my eyes adjust.

you go on

living your life,

and

I will live mine.

you know I love you

how much do you carry

for a sliver of happiness?

you are sweet, painfully patient,

how could I ask you

to undo yourself for me?

worse, that you stay,

even when you see the price it costs

us both.

love isn't about convenience

you insist,

as though I am brave enough

to do what we need.

close my eyes,

say things I don't mean,

when it gets too real,

when you ask for more

than I can give.

it is easier that way,

to keep on loving you

pretend it does not

wear us down.

cat and mouse

would the world explode if

you told me you loved me?

you sit on my couch and

you cross your arms.

your hand on my back,

pointing out my favourite constellations,

a hot cup of tea when I'm sick,

your heartbeat against mine, slow and
steady.

you can't get the words out.

not like me -

they

tumble

out.

you tell me I'm too open

I should guard my heart.

I tell you I'd rather be honest

and get hurt,

than let a good thing pass by.

I take a step forward,

you take a step back.

I go to leave,

you ask me to stay.

you touch me and it feels like fire. it hurts
and it feels like home.

if it doesn't hurt then it isn't worth it. how
can it be real if I don't ache?

you ask me to stay and I never say no.

maybe next time, I will.

I hope I will.

eye masks

I dream of small, good moments with you.

dreams where you place your head on my lap.

our apartment is warm from endless sunlight.

curtains flutter from the breeze.

honeysuckle grows on our balcony,
intertwining vines with buzzing bees.

dreams where we walk on the beach,

blue water lapping at our feet,

we look for brightly coloured shells to dry later,

I kiss you and you taste of salt.

we find sand in the corners of our home,
our shower,

we change our sheets

only then can we sleep.

dreams where we sit in meadows I have
only ever seen photos of,

in a country I have only ever seen on a
map.

your eyes are so green, your smile so soft,

full of tenderness and possibility.

oil and vinegar

(falling)

you're unlike anyone I've

ever met,

my world

blurs.

(falling in love)

we drive until sunset,

watch the rain pour down

in the back of your car.

(falling in love again)

I didn't know hunger until I met you

stricken by

equal parts desire and repulsion

held hostage.

(and again)

that familiar stirring in my chest

(oh, no)

if I tell you,

will you crumble

under my touch?

you say,

don't break the spell,

and hold my hand

like that's enough.

the water is warm

water slides off her,

sly and beautiful nymph,

beckons you closer with

webbed hands.

the water is warm,

she says.

see how it waits for you?

rainbows dance across the surface,

you do not see them

for what they are:

snakes.

you come closer

she smiles,

sharp teeth and

pretty pink lips,

heart clenches,

you would do anything

for that smile.

you take her hand and

she laughs,

bells chiming in the breeze.

she pulls you under,

so close.

she was right, you think,

even as your lungs burn.

the water is warm.

hello, operator

you're the train that never leaves the
station,

I'm sitting there, waiting.

my friends beg me to buy another ticket,

go to any other destination.

how could I,

when I have already purchased this ticket,

non-refundable.

the operator says,

delayed

delayed

delayed

just in case,

I'll stay a while longer yet.

it was sunny yesterday

always

one mistake away

from losing you.

watching your face

for clues.

what will it be today?

what does the forecast say?

is a storm on the way?

wary of what I

say,

do.

wary of what I don't.

always

a 10% chance of rain but

no thunder today.

shoulders drop,

big breath out.

no umbrella,

if it rains and I get drenched,

should've known

the forecast better.

tigris

full moon lights up my room

in the moonlight you

glow

I'm not sure where I end and

you begin

your claws, sharp teeth,

blend into my skin.

when you leave

vanilla clings to my pillows, my sheets,

feels like you didn't really leave at all.

I dream of you,

sitting on the edge of my bed,

looking back at me.

blood on your tongue,

my tigris

in the morning, you tell me you dreamt of me,

getting lost on the way to you.

in my dreams you're never lost,

entirely mine,

yet in my dreams, somehow,

I am still my own.

a lot can happen in the dark

wait until the sun sets

then you slink inside

you hold me like I was made for you

so right I break in two

living moment to moment

it's torture, I know

will you wait

until I'm ready?

I'm yours

behind closed doors

until the sun comes up

I'm yours.

loving her in private

she stands amidst the sunflowers, red hair
aglow against pale blue skies.

back to me, a halo envelopes her. I take a
photo, she is my angel in that passing
moment.

I wish she would stay that way forever, so
as to not have to face her, not watch her
heart break.

she does not call me a coward, but I see it
on her face.

do not be ashamed, she tells me. she calls
me beautiful, kisses me softly. I do not
deserve it. the cross against my neck burns
at her touch.

browsing for snacks at the grocery store, I
pause before the sunflower seeds.

it was summers ago that we stood in that
field, sundresses and bare feet in the soil.
the fullness of her mouth and

the freckles across her cheeks. the softness
of her stomach and the scent of vanilla.
my sweet summer breeze.

I think of how much she meant to me,
how much it mattered. church pews,
passing looks, unanswered questions. how
I wish it had mattered less.

I watch tv with my husband. I crack the
seeds between my teeth and wish I had let
her matter to me more.

the tourist

you are

sweet and patient

open a drawer for me,

take off my weary shoes.

unsure

if I love you or I'm just passing through

if I did

what would father say?

suitcase is packed

kiss me goodbye?

breaking your heart,

breaking mine too.

he waits at the station

kiss him hello

doesn't taste like vanilla

or flutter my heart.

I unpack,

father sighs in relief.

close my eyes,

picture your face.

is it too late,

to buy a ticket and go back to you?

empty space

does it matter

who is sleeping next to you

so long as you are not alone?

cold cup of tea

fuel tank half empty

they blend together

fat thin tall short blonde brunette

close your eyes and reach for

a stranger

relief

to fill the space you left behind.

pomegranate seeds

ruby stains across my teeth,

you hand me more for me to eat.

so sweet,

your hands tinted red from the effort

of seducing me.

won't you stay?

so dark, down here,

but

you'd be here with me.

I'll take away the cold,

the hunger,

you say,

a promise, or a chain?

I ache,

so wary,

just give in.

but my heart, my soul,

they long for spring.

the tether

the devil's lap is familiar,

so very warm.

around your wrists,

golden handcuffs

weigh you down, like lead.

so tired,

you cannot remember the last time

you felt rested.

so tired,

you cannot remember the last time

you were honest.

he gives you mulled wine

fog fills your head.

one night, you decline,

you've had enough.

catharsis,

at finding the words you were so scared to say.

catharsis,

at letting the handcuffs melt away.

dawn at long last

all night long,

we sat and talked,

your hand in mine.

patient and tender,

coaxing me out of my

shell.

you tell me,

why say yes,

when you mean no?

you're right,

a window, unlocked.

sweet sunrise,

tendrils of light disrupting

the dark.

at last

the mirror does not scare me

and the day

is warm enough to step into.

how slowly the night

loosens its grip

the shadows' teeth

no longer seem

so sharp

were they ever?

Part III

The Sun

the past is not the future

when I was a child

my parents read bedtime stories

where the princess fell in love with the prince.

everything would be fixed

through the blinding light of love.

I waited, for my own prince,

to sweep me off my feet

and wash away my sins,

make me whole.

a story is just a story.

let me write a new one:

let me hold my own hand,

and forgive myself

for those supposed sins.

I stand on my balcony

and catch a star falling

in my palms.

it burns and so I let it go.

I give myself permission

to let it all

go.

sunflowers

plant a seed

watch it unfurl

remember to water

and use fertiliser

dirt under your nails

heat on your face

some days you forget,

worry that your guilt will

bleed out,

poison the soil

the seed is forgiving

it will still burst through

and turn its

heavy face to the sun.

kintsugi

my home is a museum

of everyone I have ever loved

and who has loved me.

a ceramic candlestick we bought at a market

holds a beeswax candle

golden cracks down the side

after everything

she still glows.

you introduced me to gardening.

I grow tomatoes,

because they bring me joy.

what better reason to do something,

than to bring myself joy?

the tomatoes grow wild,

absorbing the sun,

plentiful fruit.

sweet red reminders

that what is broken may be mended

and what is planted

can flourish.

pass me the map

so caught up in loving you,

I forgot to love myself,

compass tucked away in a pocket.

maybe it was easier

to love you more,

break my own heart

before you could

and yet, through loving you,

I found a mirror I cannot escape.

reflected in your big blue eyes

feelings I cannot outrun

all my worries,

both dampened and brought to life

through your touch.

terrifying

and freeing

stand still, for just a moment,

that's all I need to do,

let the needle settle.

my own true north.

cherry blossoms

spring, at last!

let life's wonder

kiss me on the mouth

remind me of the good!

acceptance

I used to wait by the phone,

count the nights until I would see you again.

twirl my hair and

imagine us as something kinder,

how it could be,

if only things were different.

if only I was better.

if only you loved me more.

now I build a life

for myself.

count the minutes until my tea is brewed,

dream about the things I will do,

the places I will visit.

embroidery decorates the walls,

with motifs of spring.

and at night,

my home no longer feels empty.

how can it,

when I am there?

austin

white fur on every sweater

paw print embedded on my heart

he curls up in the middle of the bed

gentle snoring

cover him with a blanket,

lipstick kisses on his head

he stretches out

curls up again

so angelic in his sleep

some days I still see

the imprint of his body

on the middle of my bed.

leave them be

you will pluck the stars from the sky

and hand me the moon on a silver platter.

I would rather

leave them be

and lay my weary head

on a soft pillow

while sun rays

kiss my cheeks.

tea bags

black tea, over-brewed

even a spoonful of honey

won't fix it now

your mouth on mine

cherry lip balm

sickly sweet words you don't mean

pour out the tea

and decline your call,

let the bitterness go.

all's well that ends well

afternoon sun,

cheap coffee,

stale croissant,

she sits on the park bench and smiles.

turns off her phone,

dips her croissant in the coffee,

opens her romance book,

and steps into a different world.

evening breeze pulls her back,

rested and relaxed,

she closes her book.

hand in hand

with her own shadow,

she reads the night sky and

follows the constellations

all the way home.

Acknowledgements

Thank you to everyone who helped bring this book to life.

To my mum, for her endless words of encouragement.

To my friends, for their support and excitement.

To everyone who has loved me, and who I have loved in return, for inspiring me to create.

Line art illustrations designed by FreePik.

About the Author

Daniela Koulikov is a writer with a background in human rights and journalism. She loves the stories people share and how they connect to the world around them.

When she isn't writing or brewing earl grey, she is exploring identity and desire through literature. She finds joy in the company of animals and in helping where she can.

She lives in Australia.

This is her debut poetry collection.

www.ingramcontent.com/pod-product-compliance
Lightning Source LLC
La Vergne TN
LVHW051015080826
845145LV00009B/2638
9781764623100